D1553339

AN INTRODUCTION TO CONTRACT DRAFTING

SECOND EDITION

■ ■ ■

By

William K. Sjostrom, Jr.
Professor of Law
James E. Rogers College of Law
The University of Arizona

WEST₀

Mat #41405009

© 2012 Thomson Reuters
© 2013 LEG, Inc. d/b/a West Academic Publishing
610 Opperman Drive
St. Paul, MN 55123
1-800-313-9378
Printed in the United States of America

ISBN: 978–0–314–28723–6

TABLE OF CONTENTS

AN INTRODUCTION TO CONTRACT DRAFTING

SECOND EDITION

An Introduction to Contract Drafting

I.   OVERVIEW

Contract drafting is an important skill to have in your toolkit, and it is indispensible for a transactional attorney.[1] It is a skill that takes time to develop, and the best way to do so is through drafting and reviewing contracts. This Introduction discusses some basic concepts of contract drafting to help you develop this important skill. At the end are some exercises to (1) get you to apply and expand on the covered concepts, and (2) give you a chance to review and draft some contracts.

II.   CONTRACT COMPONENTS

Contract drafting is a unique type of writing. While the objective of most legal writing is either to persuade or convey information, neither of these objectives is the primary goal of a contract. The primary goal of a con-

---

[1] A transactional attorney (also called a corporate attorney) works on transactions or deals and not cases. Examples of deals include big things like the acquisition of another business, selling stock to the public, or borrowing a large sum of money from a bank and more routine things like supply agreements, services agreements, and equipment leases. A transactional attorney advises the client as to the best way to structure a deal, negotiates the legal terms of the deal, and drafts or reviews the contract(s) to document the deal.

tract is to set forth the terms of the contracting parties' agreement in language that will be interpreted by all subsequent readers in exactly the same way. This goal is achieved through precise and clear drafting.

Because all contracts have the same basic goal, most contracts are comprised of the same types of provisions regardless of subject matter or complexity. This section provides an overview of these provisions and is divided into three subsections: universal provisions, delayed closing provisions, and continuing relationship provisions. Before reading on, you may want to skim the contract included with Exercise 1 at the end of this Introduction to familiarize yourself with a contract and get a sense for how the various provisions fit together.

A.   UNIVERSAL PROVISIONS

Universal provisions are provisions typically included in all contracts. I describe nine different types below.

1. Title

The title of a contract appears centered at the top of the first page. Oftentimes it is in all caps and bold. To aid the reader, a contract's title should reflect the subject matter of the contract. The title should be concise but not generic. Titling a contract "Agreement" conveys nothing to the reader. Titling a contract "Lease Agreement" is a little better but raises the question of what's being leased. "Office Lease Agreement" is even better (assuming the contract is for the lease of an office). Note that it is customary to use the word "Agreement" in the title instead of "Contract."

2. Preamble

The preamble (sometimes called the introductory paragraph) is the first paragraph of a contract appearing just under the title. It repeats the title of the contract and then sets forth the date of the contract and the parties to the contract. Here is a sample preamble:

> Office Lease Agreement, dated August 1, 2010, between Apex Property, LLC, a Delaware limited liability company ("<u>Landlord</u>"), and Maude G. Flanders, an individual residing at 1131 Green Street, Tucson, Arizona 85718 ("<u>Tenant</u>").

You should use full legal names when specifying the names of the parties. For an individual, the custom is to follow the person's name with "an individual" to signify the party is not an entity and to include the person's address to distinguish the party from some other person with the same name. For an entity party, you should use the entity's official legal name as specified in the entity's organizational document. Pay attention to punctuation (or lack thereof). For example, if a limited liability company's articles of organization state that the company's name is "Apex Property, LLC" make sure you include the comma after "Property" but do not put a period after the "L" the "L" or the "C." The custom is to follow an entity party's name with its jurisdiction of organization to distinguish the party from an entity with the same name organized in some other jurisdiction.

You should use parentheses to indicate defined terms. For example, in the sample preamble above, the use of parentheses indicates that "Landlord" and "Tenant" are defined terms (I discuss defined terms in greater detail in Section IV.B.2 below).

Some lawyers prefer to draft the preamble as a sentence to make it easier to read. For example, the preamble from above could be redrafted as follows:

This Office Lease Agreement *is* dated August 1, 2010, and *is* between Apex Property, LLC, a Delaware limited liability company ("<u>Landlord</u>"), and Maude G. Flanders, an individual residing at 1131 Green Street, Tucson, Arizona 85718 ("<u>Tenant</u>"). (emphasis added)

---

3. Recitals

Recitals (also called background) explain why the parties are entering into the contract. Their purpose is to provide context for the reader. Here are sample recitals from a trademark license agreement:

RECITALS:

A.   Licensor possesses rights in the "RANGER" trademark covering boats manufactured under such trademark.

B.   Licensee desires a license to use the trademark on non-motorized miniature toy boats and related miniature boat accessories to be manufactured and sold by Licensee, and Licensor is willing to grant such a license to Licensee.

You should not include any substantive provisions (those addressing rights or obligations of the parties) in the recitals. All substantive provisions should be in the body of the contract. Lawyers often omit recitals from short and simple contracts.

4. Words of Agreement

Words of agreement (also called the lead-in) come after the recitals and right before the contract's body. Here are some examples:

Accordingly, the parties agree as follows:

or, if the contract does not contain recitals,

The parties agree as follows:

It is fairly common for words of agreement to include a recitation of consideration such as "in consideration of the following terms, covenants, and conditions; and other good and valuable consideration, the receipt and sufficiency of which is hereby acknowledged. . ." This language generally has no legal effect because the recital of consideration does not save a contract that is not actually supported by consideration. Thus, you should omit it to shorten the lead-in and improve readability.

5. Performance Provision

A performance provision contains the parties' promises to perform whatever it is they will be doing under the contract. Here is an example from a supply agreement:

> <u>Purchase and Sale of Products</u>. Subject to the provisions of this Agreement, Supplier shall sell to Buyer, and Buyer shall purchase from Supplier, all of Buyer's requirements for Products.

6. Consideration Provision

A consideration provision specifies what one party is paying in exchange for the other party's performance. Here an example from a consulting agreement:

> Compensation. The Company shall pay Consultant $250.00 per hour of services rendered by Consultant under this Agreement.

7. Representations and Warranties

Representations and warranties, or reps for short, are assertions of fact by the contracting parties. They generally serve one of two purposes: (1) to ensure that a party either receives what the party is expecting to receive under the contract or has a breach of contract claim against the other party; and/or (2) to allocate the risk of an unknown fact to one of the parties. For example, when purchasing a used car it is probably a good idea to include in the purchase agreement, among other things, a representation and warranty that the car's odometer reflects the actual number of miles the car has been driven. Here is an example:

> Seller represents and warrants to Buyer as follows:
>
> (a) The Car's odometer reads 33,340 miles, which is the actual number of miles the Car has been driven.

If it turns out that the car's odometer has been rolled back, then Buyer did not get the car he expected (one with 33,340 miles on it). However, Buyer will have a breach of contract claim against Seller because the representation and warranty Seller made to Buyer is false. In other words, the representation and warranty has allocated the risk of the odometer being inaccurate to Seller because Buyer has recourse against Seller if it turns out to be inaccurate. Conversely, if the contract was silent on the car's odometer reading, Buyer would be implicitly assuming the risk of an inaccurate odometer. In such a case, Buyer would not have any recourse against Seller under the contract because Seller did not represent and warrant to Buyer that the odometer reflected the actual miles driven.

Whether Seller agrees to include the above representation and warranty in the contract will likely be the subject of negotiations between the parties and may impact other parts of the contract. For example, the parties may initially agree on a sale price of $12,000. However, when Buyer insists on getting an odometer representation and warranty from Seller, Seller may agree to provide it only if Buyer agrees to pay $12,250 for the car. Essentially, Buyer would pay Seller an additional $250 for Seller assuming the inaccurate odometer risk.

Alternatively, Seller could agree to provide the representation and warranty if it contains a knowledge qualifier. In such a case, the language would read "The Car's odometer reads 33,340 miles, which, to *Seller's knowledge,* is the actual number of miles the Car has been driven." Under this language, Buyer is protected if Seller knows the odometer has been rolled back but has withheld this information from Seller. However, Buyer is not protected if it turns out that the odometer has been rolled back but Seller had no knowledge of it.

8. General Provisions

General provisions (also called miscellaneous or boilerplate provisions) appear at the end of a contract and address assorted issues related to the contract. Here are some examples of general provisions:

(a) <u>Entire Agreement</u>. This Agreement is the final, complete, and exclusive statement of the parties' agreement on the matters contained in this Agreement and supersedes all related prior communications, understandings and agreements between the parties.

(b) <u>Governing Law</u>. This Agreement, and the respective rights of the parties under this Agreement, shall be governed by and construed under the laws of Arizona, without regard to such state's conflict of law principles.

(c) <u>Amendments</u>. This Agreement may be amended only by a writing signed by each party to this Agreement.

Lawyers include an entire agreement provision (also known as a merger or integration provision) in light of the parol evidence rule. The provision establishes that the contract is final and complete and therefore cannot be contradicted or supplemented by prior or contemporaneous agreements. At the time of contracting, it is generally in both parties' interest to limit the terms of the deal to the written contract.

Lawyers include a governing law provision (also known as a choice of law provision) to foreclose future disputes between the parties as to which state's laws are to govern the contract. If such a provision is not included, the general rule is that the law of the state with the most substantial relationship to the transaction governs, and the parties may disagree on which state that is. Choosing the state also allows the parties to tailor the contract to the laws of the specified state, if necessary. The "without regard to such state's conflict of law principles" language is to handle *renvoi* or where state A's conflict of laws principles dictate that a court should apply state B's laws, but state B's conflict of laws principles dictate that a court should apply state A's laws.

Lawyers include an amendments provision in an effort to avoid a party later claiming the other party agreed to an oral modification of the contract. Various courts, however, have allowed oral modifications notwithstanding such a clause, so the clause is not definitive on this issue.

You should probably include the above three general provisions in any contract you draft. There are many other general provisions that you will see in contracts. Examples include notice, waiver of jury trial, severability, successors and assigns, and counterparts. Whether you should include additional general provisions depends on a number of considerations including the type of contract, the amount of money involved, and custom.

9. Concluding Clause and Signature Blocks

Most contracts end with a concluding clause followed by signature blocks. Here is an example:

> To evidence the parties' agreement to this Agreement, they have signed it on the date stated in the preamble.
>
> **Apex Property, LLC**
>
> By: *Homer J. Simpson*
>
> Its: *President*
>
> *Maude G. Flanders*
> Maude G. Flanders

Because Apex Property, LLC is not a natural person, an officer or some other agent has to sign on its behalf. In the above, example, Apex's president, Homer J. Simpson,

signed. Note that the person signs on the
"By" line and writes his or her position on
the "Its" line. For an individual, you simply
insert a line and type the individuals name
under it. The names in the signature blocks
should match the names specified in the contract's preamble.

B. DELAYED CLOSING PROVISIONS

Delayed closing provisions are provisions
included in a contract because the parties
will be signing the contract on day x but not
closing the deal until day y. A closing is
when the parties exchange consideration.
For example, the purchase of a home typically involves a delayed closing. The parties
sign a real estate purchase agreement on
day x but do not exchange consideration
(purchase price for title to the home), or
close, until day y. As a result, the contract
will need to address issues that may arise
during the period between signing and closing (often called the "gap period"). I refer to
provisions addressing delayed closing and
gap period issues as delayed closing provisions. Note that it is simpler, but not always
possible, to sign a contract and simultane-
ously exchange consideration because then
there will be no need for delayed closing provisions.

1. Closing Specifics

A closing specifics provision specifies when and where the closing is to occur. Here is an example:

> <u>Closing</u>. The Closing shall take place at the offices of Weil, Gotshal & Manges LLP, 767 Fifth Avenue, New York, New York 10153 at 9:00 a.m. Eastern Standard Time on April 1, 2013, or at such other time and place as the Company and Purchaser mutually agree.

Back in the day, at least for bigger dollar amount deals, parties to a contract and their attorneys would all gather around a table, typically in a law firm conference room, and sign the various closing documents. These days, in-person closings are somewhat rare. Instead, each party will messenger or overnight executed signature pages for the documents they need to sign. If the documents are not finalized when a party sends signature pages, the custom is for the attorney handling the closing to hold the signature pages in escrow until the documents are finalized and the signing party gives the go ahead to release them.

Depending on the type of deal, many attorneys are comfortable closing with faxed or emailed executed signature pages with the understanding that originals will be promptly sent. Each party usually signs multiple copies of closing documents (with the exception of negotiable instruments such as stock certificates and promissory notes) so that all parties and their attorneys have a set of originals.

2. Closing Deliveries

A closing deliveries provision specifies what each party must deliver to the other party at the closing (signed documents, money, keys, etc.). Here's an example from a stock purchase agreement:

<u>Closing Deliveries</u>. At the Closing the Purchaser shall deliver to the Seller the Purchase Price, and the Seller shall deliver to the Purchaser the certificates representing the Shares.

3. Covenants

A covenant is simply a promise to do or not to do something (a covenant to do something is often referred to as an "affirmative covenant" and one not to do something as a "negative covenant"). Lawyers use covenants to address, among other things, issues that may come up during the gap period.

For example, one reason the purchase of a home typically involves a delayed closing is because the buyer usually needs to obtain financing in order to close. However, in this situation, a seller may be concerned that a buyer will drag his or her feet in obtaining financing or sour on the house and purposely not pursue financing. To address this issue, a lawyer could include a financing covenant in the contract. Here's an example:

Buyer shall use Buyer's best efforts to obtain a loan within thirty days of the date of this Agreement sufficient to enable Buyer to pay Seller the Purchase Price at Closing.

Similarly, the buyer may be concerned that the seller will fail to properly maintain the property during the gap period. To address this issue, a lawyer could include the following covenant in the contract:

Seller shall maintain and, if necessary, repair the Premises so that at Closing all heating, cooling, mechanical, plumbing, and electrical systems and all built-in appliances are in working condition.

Covenants do not guarantee that the party will do (or not do) what the party promised, but they do provide the other party with a breach of contract claim in the event the covenant is not met. In addition, a breached covenant will likely give the non-breaching party an option to not close (as discussed in the next subsection).

4. Closing Conditions

Closing conditions specify conditions that must be fulfilled or waived before a party is obligated to close on the transaction. Here are some examples:

> <u>Conditions to Buyer's Obligations</u>. Buyer's obligation to close the Sale is subject to the satisfaction of the following conditions:
>
> (a) <u>Representations and Warranties</u>. Seller's representations and warranties must be true on the Closing Date.
>
> (b) <u>Covenants</u>. Seller must have performed all of the covenants to be performed by it on or before the Closing Date.

Notice that the above closing conditions are tied to representation and warranties and covenants made by Seller elsewhere in the contract. Consequently, if a representation and warranty turns out to be false (even if true when the contract was signed) or Seller fails to comply with one of its covenants, Buyer would not have to close on the transaction.

Oftentimes a contract that contemplates a delayed closing will also include a provision that allows one or both parties to unilaterally terminate the contract if the closing conditions have not been fulfilled or waived by a specified date (often called a drop-dead date). See section II.C.2. below for a discussion of termination provisions.

5. General Provisions

In addition to the general provisions described in II.A.7. above (entire agreement,
governing law, amendments), a contract that
contemplates a delayed closing should include a waiver provision because it is not
uncommon for a party to waive a minor failure to comply with a covenant or some other
provision of the contract. Here's an example:

> <u>Waiver</u>. No purported waiver of any provision of
> this Agreement shall be binding unless set forth
> in a writing signed by the party to be charged.
> Any waiver shall be limited to the circumstance
> or event specifically referenced in the written
> waiver document and shall not be deemed a
> waiver of any other term of this Agreement or
> of the same circumstance or event upon any re-
> currence thereof.

As discussed above, formal closings where
the parties gather around a table and sign
on the same signature page are increasingly
rare. Instead, signature pages are signed in
counterparts. For example, say a closing
document contained the signature block
from section II.A.9. above. It is likely that
Apex's attorney will overnight, email, or fax
Homer a copy of the signature page for
Homer to sign. At roughly the same time,
Maude's attorney will likewise overnight,
email, or fax a copy of the signature page for
her to sign. As a result, the parties' signa-

tures will not appear on the same copy of the signature page. To address this situation, it is common to include a "Counterparts" provision. Here's an example:

<u>Counterparts</u>. This Agreement may be executed in one or more counterparts, each of which shall be deemed an original, but all of which taken together constitute only one agreement. Delivery of an executed counterpart of a signature page to this Agreement by fax or e-mail shall be effective as delivery of a manually executed counterpart of this Agreement.

Notice that the provision also addresses the issue of faxed or e-mailed signature pages.

C. CONTINUING RELATIONSHIP PROVISIONS

Continuing relationship provisions are provisions included in a contract because the performance of one or both parties will be occurring over a period of time. For example, a twelve-month apartment lease may require the tenant to pay rent each month and the landlord to maintain the apartment over the term of the lease.

1. Covenants

As mentioned above, a covenant is a promise to do or not to do something. Covenants are important in the continuing relationship context because they address how the parties are to act during the term of the contract. For example, a year-long consulting contract may include the following covenant:

> Consultant shall perform the consulting services in a professional manner and to the Company's reasonable satisfaction.

This covenant does not guarantee that Consultant will do a good job, but if coupled with a termination provision, as discussed next, this covenant will serve as a way for the Company to get out of the contract early if it is unhappy with the Consultant's work.

2. Term and Termination

A term provision specifies when the contract begins and ends. Here's an example:

> Term. Unless terminated earlier in accordance with the terms of this Agreement, this Agreement shall commence on April 1, 2010 and shall continue until May 31, 2013.

A termination provision allows one or both of the parties to terminate the agreement early, that is, before the term has run. Here's an example:

Termination. The Company may terminate this Agreement upon ten days written notice to Consultant following any breach of this Agreement by Consultant.

Thus, for example, say a consulting agreement included the above termination provision and a covenant that "Consultant shall perform the consulting services in a professional manner." If Consultant's performance is unprofessional, Consultant would be in breach of the covenant and therefore in breach of the Agreement. Thus, the Company would be able to terminate the Agreement early pursuant to the termination provision.

3. General Provisions

In addition to the general provisions described above (entire agreement, governing law, amendments, and waiver), a contract that contemplates a continuing relationship between the parties should address assignment and delegation. Here's a sample provision from a consulting agreement that covers both issues:

> <u>Assignment and Delegation</u>. Consultant has neither the right nor the power to assign any of Consultant's rights or delegate any of Consultant's duties under this Agreement by operation of the law or otherwise without the prior written consent of the Company. Any attempt to assign or delegate without this consent is void.

This provision prevents Consultant from subcontracting (delegating) his or her duties under the contract (e.g., providing consulting service to the Company) to a third party without the Company's consent. It would also likewise prevent Consultant from assigning his or her payment rights under the contract (i.e., his or her right to the compensation specified in the contract for providing consulting services) without the consent of the Company. A common error made by practicing attorneys is to include a provision that prohibits assignment without consent but fails to address delegation. As you may have learned in your contracts class, assignment and delegation are related but distinct concepts—a party assigns rights and delegates duties. Therefore, as in the sample above, a contract should normally address both concepts.

III.   MANAGING RISK

Some of the provisions and language lawyers use in contracts are designed to manage risk. I touched on risk management in section II.A.7. above when discussing how representations and warranties allocate the risk of an unknown fact to one party or the other. I cover some other common risk management mechanisms in this section. Unlike the contract components I covered in part II., you will not necessarily include all (or any) of the below provisions in a contract. It usually depends on which party you represent and its bargaining power.

A. LIMITATION OF LIABILITY

A limitation of liability provision limits the liability of a party to a contract to a specified amount. Here is some sample language from a supply agreement:

> In no event will Seller's liability for any claim, whether in contract, tort, or any other theory of liability, exceed the total price paid by Buyer to Seller for the Products.

Absent this sort of language, a breaching Seller would generally be on the hook to Buyer for expectation damages (money damages in an amount sufficient to place Buyer in the position it would have been in had Seller not breached) even if these damages exceed the amount received by Seller under the agreement. Thus, it is clearly a seller/service provider favorable provision that typically would not be included in an agreement drafted by a buyer's counsel. If a buyer acquiesces to including a limitation of liability provision in the contract, it should at least seek as high a cap as possible, for example, some multiple of amounts paid under the contract.

B. DAMAGE DISCLAIMER

A damage disclaimer provision limits the type of damages a party can receive following a contract breach by the other party. Here is sample language from a consulting agreement:

IN NO EVENT WILL CONSULTANT BE LIABLE TO THE COMPANY FOR ANY SPECIAL, INCIDENTAL OR CONSEQUENTIAL DAMAGES FOR ANY BREACH OF THIS AGREEMENT, EVEN IF ADVISED OF THE POSSIBILITY OF SUCH DAMAGES.

Absent this sort of language, a breaching Consultant would potentially be on the hook to the Company for things like lost profits resulting from the beach. Once again, this is a seller/service provider favorable provision.

Note that if a seller asks for a damage disclaimer and/or a limitation of liability provision (they often go hand and hand) but the buyer objects, it is typical for the seller to agree to make the provisions reciprocal. This means drafting these provisions so that they apply to both the seller and the buyer. Here's the above damage disclaimer redrafted to be reciprocal (I have underlined the new language):

IN NO EVENT WILL <u>EITHER PARTY</u> BE LI-ABLE TO <u>THE OTHER PARTY</u> FOR ANY SPECIAL, INCIDENTAL OR CONSEQUEN-TIAL DAMAGES FOR ANY BREACH OF THIS AGREEMENT, EVEN IF ADVISED OF THE POSSIBILITY OF SUCH DAMAGES.

This may seem like a fair compromise, but it is likely of little value to a buyer whose only obligation under the contract is to pay for the goods/services provided. This is because it is highly unlikely that damages recoverable by a seller for buyer's failure to pay will ever exceed the amount owed by buyer plus interest. In other words, buyer will have to pay the same amount in damages whether the contract does or does not include a reciprocal limitation of liability provision and damage disclaimer.

A damage disclaimer is often drafted in all caps, as in the above samples. This is to make it conspicuous which helps rebut a later claim that the provision is unenforceable because it is unconscionable.

C. INDEMNIFICATION

An indemnification provision obligates a party to cover specified costs and expenses incurred by the other party. Here is sample language from a supply agreement:

> Supplier will indemnify Buyer from any claims, suits, actions, proceedings (formal or informal), investigations, judgments, deficiencies, demands, damages, settlements, liabilities, reasonable attorney's fees, as and when incurred, arising out of, in connection with, or based upon any Products sold under this Agreement.

Thus, for example, say Supplier, a tire manufacturer, sold Buyer tires for the golf carts Buyer manufactures, and that "Products" in the above language is defined to include these tires. Some of the tires were defective, and as a result a purchaser of one of Buyer's golf carts is seriously injured when a tire fails and the cart flips. Hence, the golf cart purchaser brings a products liability suit against Buyer. Supplier would be contractually obligated to cover the costs of Buyer's defense and any resulting damage award or settlement because the suit "arises out of" Products (the defective tires) sold under the Agreement. The basic idea is to shield one party from mistakes or misconduct of the other party.

Absent the above sort of language, Buyer may have a breach of contract claim against Supplier, especially if the Agreement included a rep by Supplier that all Products sold under the Agreement were free from defects. However, any limitation of liability or damage waiver in the contract would likely apply (in that regard, the agreement should be explicit on whether such provisions apply to indemnification obligations), and Supplier would not necessarily have to pay Buyer's costs as incurred (such as legal fees) as required under the indemnification provision.

Unlike reciprocal limitation of liability provisions and damage disclaimers, reciprocal indemnification provisions are not necessarily favorable to one party or the other. For example, Supplier could get sued even if its tires were not defective but Buyer negligently installed them. In that case, it would be beneficial to Supplier if Buyer contractually agreed to indemnify it. As a result, if for example, Buyer insists on the above indemnification provision, Supplier would typically insist that a similar provision pursuant to which Buyer is obligated to indemnify Supplier also be included. Thus, before including or asking for an indemnification provision for your client, you should consider the likelihood of your client invoking it versus having to pay out under one. In other words, it may be better for your client not to bring up the issue.

D. INSURANCE

An indemnification provision is often coupled with an insurance requirement. Here is sample language:

Seller shall keep in full force and effect at all times, a public liability insurance policy or policies with coverage for both products and completed operations, containing blanket contractual liability coverage insuring all written contracts of Seller and naming Buyer as an additional insured, written by an insurance carrier acceptable to Buyer in aggregate amounts required by Buyer which shall not be less than $1 million per occurrence, combined single limit, bodily injury and property damage. Seller will deliver to Buyer a completed certificate of insurance on forms approved by Buyer and signed by an authorized representative of the insurance carrier(s) certifying that such insurance coverage has been issued, is in full force, naming Buyer as an additional insured, and that if such insurance is cancelled or changed so as to affect the coverage, at least thirty (30) days prior written notice of such cancellation or change will be sent to Buyer.

The basic idea is to have another pocket available in case a party suffers a loss because of faulty products or services provided by the other party and the other party is not financially able to meet its indemnification obligations or pay a judgment against it.

The required policy limits ($1 million in the example above), types of coverage, and other terms are subject to negotiations between the parties and vary depending on the subject matter of the deal. For example, an insurance provision in a services agreement should require the service provider to have professional liability insurance which covers losses from errors and omissions in the performance of the services.

E.   FORCE MAJEURE

A force majeure provision excuses a party from liability if it is unable to perform its obligations under a contract because of the occurrence of a specified event. Here is some sample language from a supply agreement:

Seller shall not be liable for any failure to deliver or any delay in delivery which shall be caused, directly or indirectly, and in whole or in part, by fire; flood; rain or windstorm; explosion; machinery or equipment breakdown; sabotage; strike or work stoppages; civil disturbances; war (whether or not officially declared); voluntary or mandatory compliance with any law, regulation, ruling or policy of any branch of federal, state, or local government; shortages of labor, raw materials, equipment, fuel or power; transportation delays or unavailability; any act of God; late receipt of order or of full manufacturing details; failure of Buyer and Seller to agree on final product specifications; or any other cause beyond the reasonable control of Seller. In any such event, Seller shall use its best efforts to equitably allocate available materials covered by this agreement among its customers, including Buyer.

Absent this sort of language, if, for example, Seller was unable to perform because its plant was flooded, it would have to argue that its performance was excused under the common law doctrine of impracticability. If this argument failed, Seller would be liable to Buyer for breach of contract. Hence, the basic idea behind a force majeure provision is to broaden the scope of events beyond those falling under the doctrine of impracticability that will excuse a party's failure to perform under a contract.

As with a limitation of liability provision and damage disclaimer, if a buyer objects to including a force majeure provision, it is typical for the seller to offer to make the provision reciprocal. Here is an example of a reciprocal force majeure provision:

> No party to this Agreement will be liable to any other party or be in breach of this Agreement due to any event of force majeure or other event beyond its reasonable control; including, without limitation, strikes, shortages of or inability to secure labor, fuel, energy, materials or supplies at reasonable prices or from regular sources, transportation delays, riots, war, fire and acts of God.

Once again, this may seem like a fair compromise, but it is likely of little value to a buyer whose only obligation under the contract is to pay for the goods/services provided. This is because it is highly unlikely that buyer will ever be able to point to a strike, inability to secure labor, war, etc. to excuse it from having to pay for the goods or services provided by seller as these events will not prevent a buyer from accessing its money.

F.   QUALIFIERS

A qualifier is language that qualifies, or softens, a rep, covenant, condition, or other contractual provision. By far the most common qualifiers are knowledge and materiality.

1. Knowledge

I introduced the use of a knowledge qualifier in section II.A.7. above when discussing representations and warranties. Here is another example of a rep with a knowledge qualifier from a real estate purchase agreement:

> To Seller's knowledge, neither the Property nor any real estate in the vicinity of the Property is in violation of any federal, state, local or administrative agency ordinance, law, rule, regulation, order or requirement relating to environmental conditions or Hazardous Material.

Under this language, Buyer is assuming the risk of an unknown environmental issue with respect to the Property. If the rep did not include "To Seller's knowledge" (lawyers would then call it a "flat" or "unqualified" rep), Seller would be assuming this risk.

It is fairly common for an agreement to define the term knowledge. Here is a sample definition:

> For purposes of this Agreement, "knowledge" means the actual knowledge of the Company's executive officers.

Note that this definition favors the maker of the rep because it is limited to actual as opposed to constructive knowledge (things they did not know but should have known).

2. Materiality

Below is a negative covenant from a loan agreement that contains a materiality qualifier.

> <u>Transfers</u>. Except for Permitted Transfers, Borrower shall not voluntarily or involuntarily transfer, sell, lease, license, lend or in any other manner convey any equitable, beneficial or legal interest in any of its material assets.

Under this language, Borrower is free to sell, lease, license, etc. immaterial assets because the materiality qualifier limits the scope of the covenant to material assets.

Here is another example:

<u>Termination</u>. The Company may terminate this Agreement upon ten days written notice to Consultant following any material breach of this Agreement by Consultant.

This example should look familiar because you saw it in Section II.C.3. above. The only difference is that I added a materiality qualifier. As a result, the Company would not be able to terminate the agreement for an immaterial breach by Consultant.

A key issue here is, of course, the meaning of "material." Contracts often do not define it, in part because it is a term that is difficult to define with precision. As a result, on occasion contracting parties will disagree as to whether something is material and the issue ends up in court. A number of courts have held that something is material if knowledge of it would affect a person's decision-making process. If this is not the definition the parties have in mind, the contract should specify a different definition such as "important enough to merit attention."

G. "EFFORTS" MODIFIERS

Contracts often include covenants the performance of which are outside of the control of the party obligated to perform. Here's an example of such a covenant from a real estate purchase agreement:

> Buyer shall obtain a loan within thirty days of the date of this Agreement sufficient to enable Buyer to pay Seller the Purchase Price at Closing.

Performance of this covenant is outside of Buyer's control because it is dependent on a third party agreeing to loan money to Buyer. Lawyers would refer to the covenant as absolute. Either Buyer gets the financing or is in breach of contract. In other words, the contract allocates to Buyer the risk associated with obtaining financing.

If Buyer is uncomfortable shouldering this risk, he or she may insist that an "efforts" modifier be added to the language. Here is the above covenant with the addition of an efforts modifier:

> Buyer shall use reasonable efforts to obtain a loan within thirty days of the date of this Agreement sufficient to enable Buyer to pay Seller the Purchase Price at Closing.

Under this language, Buyer would not be in breach of the contract if he or she failed to obtain financing so long as Buyer used reasonable efforts in trying to do so.

Lawyers use various formulations of efforts modifiers in contracts in addition to "reasonable efforts." Examples include "best efforts," "commercially reasonable efforts," "commercially reasonable best efforts," "good-faith efforts," "diligent efforts," to name a few. This raises the question of whether one formulation requires a different degree of effort than some other formulation. A corporate lawyer is likely to say that "best efforts" is the most onerous standard requiring a party to do everything in its power to achieve the specified objective even if doing so would lead to bankruptcy. He or she is also likely to say that all other phrases require something less than that but will not be able to articulate exactly what that entails or how, for example, commercially reasonable efforts differ from good-faith efforts (especially given the contractual implied covenant of good faith).

Interestingly, a number of cases have construed "best efforts" differently than as described above. Courts have stated, for example, that "'[b]est efforts' is implicitly qualified by a reasonableness test ...,"[2] "'[b]est efforts' requires that plaintiffs pursue all reasonable methods ...,"[3] and "'[b]est efforts' ... cannot mean everything possible under the sun..."[4] In other words, it looks like these courts equate best efforts with reasonable efforts.

---

[2] Coady Corp. v. Toyota Motor Distib., 361 F.3d 50, 59 (1st Cir. 2004).

[3] Kroboth v. Brent, 215 A.D.2d 813, 814 (N.Y. App. Div. 1995).

[4] Triple-A Baseball Club Assocs. v. Northeastern Baseball, Inc., 832 F.2d 214, 228 (1st Cir. 1987).

So where does this leave things for the contract drafter? First, to ensure that a court interprets "best efforts" to mean more than reasonable efforts, you should include a definition to that effect in the contract. Second, if you are reviewing a contract and it includes an undefined best efforts obligation applicable to your client, you may not want to spend a lot of capital getting it changed to "reasonable efforts" as it will likely be interpreted by a court to mean just that anyway. Instead, consider acquiescing to staying with best efforts in exchange for something more important like a materiality qualifier on a significant rep your client is making.

IV.   PRECISION AND CLARITY

As I mentioned earlier, the primary goal of a contract is to set forth the terms of the contracting parties' agreement in language that will be interpreted by all subsequent readers in exactly the same way. This goal is achieved through precise and clear drafting.

A.   PRECISION

A precise contract is one that is free from ambiguity. By ambiguity, I mean a contractual provision or term to which the contracting parties attach different meanings.

For example, you may have read the case *Frigaliment Importing Co. v. B.N.S. International Sales Corp.*, 190 F.Supp. 116 (S.D.N.Y. 1960) for your contracts class. In

that case, Frigaliment entered into two contracts with B.N.S. for the purchase of frozen
chickens. Frigaliment thought the term
chicken meant a "broiler" (a young chicken
suitable for broiling and frying). Conversely,
B.N.S. thought it meant any bird of the
chicken genus. Thus, B.N.S. shipped
Frigaliment stewing chickens. Because stewing chickens are inferior to broilers,
Frigaliment sued B.N.S. for breach of contract. As the court recognized, "the word
'chicken' standing alone is ambiguous." It
could mean a broiler or it could mean a stewing chicken, but the contract did not specify.
Hence, presumably the dispute could have
been avoided had the contract drafter simply
included a more precise description of what
B.N.S. was to ship, saving the parties the
time and expense of litigation and preserv-
ing an amicable business relationship.

Learning to draft with precision is a skill
developed over time through working with
contracts. Here is what I mean. Let's assume
you are assigned the task of drafting a contract for the sale of frozen chickens but have
never read or heard about *Frigaliment*.
Hence, you make the same mistake that was
made in that case and use the term "chick-
en" instead of more precise terminology like
"a young chicken suitable for broiling and
frying." There is a good chance that someone
else involved with the deal (e.g., a supervising attorney, the attorney for the other side,

the client) will flag "chicken" as ambiguous (maybe because the person has read *Frigaliment* or has worked on chicken deals in the past and the issue was flagged for him or her). You will then know that "chicken" is ambiguous and use more precise terminology in your contract and all future chicken contracts you draft. In addition, you will also, hopefully, keep the ambiguity of "chicken" in mind when drafting contracts for turkey, duck, and pig deals, which will lead you to ask the client whether the contract should use more precise terminology than just "turkey," or "duck," or "pig." Over time, you will be clued in to more and more potentially ambiguous contractual language and will therefore get better and better at stripping it out of the contracts you draft and review.

B. CLARITY

A clearly drafted contract is easy, as opposed to confusing, to read. Clarity is important because if a contract is confusing to read the parties may be unable to decipher what exactly it says and therefore not realize until after it is signed that the contract does not reflect the intended deal. Contract clarity is achieved through some of the same techniques employed by various types of writers. These techniques include short sentences, active voice, logical organization, consistency, and descriptive headers. I assume you are familiar with these techniques, so I do not take them up here. Instead, I focus on two practices (one bad and one good) that impact clarity and are somewhat unique to contract drafting: the use of legalese and defined terms.

1. Legalese

Legalese is arcane and often formalistic jargon used by lawyers in contracts. Here are some contractual provisions loaded up with legalese:

AGREEMENT FOR THE CONVEYANCE OF REAL ESTATE

THIS AGREEMENT FOR THE CONVEYANCE OF REAL ESTATE is entered into this 6th day of December, 2010, by, between, and among Robert C. Smith, an individual residing at 657 Water Street, Evanston, Illinois 60209 and Jane H. Borg, an individual residing at 7 Oak Drive, Northbrook, Illinois 60601.

WITNESSETH:

WHEREAS, the party of the first part is desirous of acquiring the party of the second part's abode;

WHEREAS, the party of the second part is amendable to selling the aforementioned abode pursuant to, and in accordance with, the terms as hereinafter provided;

NOW, THEREFORE, in consideration of the sum of One Dollar ($1.00) and other good and valuable consideration, the receipt and sufficiency of the same of which is hereby acknowledged, the party of the first part and the party of the second part herewith covenant and agree as hereinafter set forth:

* * *

IN WITNESS WHEREOF the parties hereto have hereunto set their hands and seals the day and year first above written.

You may recognize the above as another example of a preamble, recitals, words of agreement, and concluding clause (see sections II.A.2., 3. & 9. above). It could (and should) be rewritten without the "whereas," "hereinafter," "hereby," and other garbage along the following lines:

HOUSE SALE AGREEMENT

This House Sale Agreement, dated December 6, 2010, is between Robert C. Smith, an individual residing at 657 Water Street, Evanston, Illinois 60209 ("Buyer") and Jane H. Borg, an individual residing at 7 Oak Drive, Northbrook, Illinois 60601 ("Seller").

Background

This agreement provides for the sale of a home by Seller to Buyer.

Accordingly, the parties agree as follows:

* * *

To evidence the parties' agreement to this Agreement, they have signed it on the date stated in the preamble.

I think everyone would agree that the rewritten version does not change the substance of the agreement but is much easier to read than the original version. I achieved this improved clarity by, for the most part, stripping out the legalese, something I strongly encourage you to do when drafting and reviewing contracts.[5]

---

[5] Use your judgment when applying this rule. For example, you may not want to cross out or rewrite all unnecessary legalese when reviewing a contract as doing so may irritate the other party's attorney making it more difficult to work with the person on the transaction or be viewed by your client (or characterized by the other side) as "over-lawyering." Because the same concerns are not present when you are doing the initial draft, you should normally strip out all legalese. However, if a senior attorney gives you a sample to start with that he or she characterizes as "good" or something similar, you may want to refrain from doing a major rewrite out of political concerns. Again, use your judgment.

2. Defined Terms

Using defined terms is a common drafting technique that enhances clarity. A defined term is a contract provision that specifies the meaning of a word or phrase used in a contract. Here's an example from a chicken purchase agreement:

> 1. **Definitions**. The following terms have the meanings assigned to them.
>
> "Chicken" means an eviscerated frozen young chicken suitable for broiling and frying.

By defining a term, the drafter can avoid having to repeat a wordy definition numerous times throughout the contract. This makes the contract easier to draft and read. Defining a term also reduces the risk of the drafter inadvertently referring to the same thing in a different way (for example, referring to "eviscerated frozen young chickens" in one place and "eviscerated frozen chickens" in another place). Using different language to cover the same concept is a major mistake because it makes it unclear whether the parties intended different concepts, and thus could give rise to litigation.

To enhance readability, select as your defined term a word or phrase that is informative and concise. For example, for "eviscerated frozen young chicken suitable for broiling and frying" use "Chicken" instead of

"EFYC" (which is concise but uninformative) or "Eviscerated Young Chicken" (which is informative but not concise).

A contract can have a separate definition section as the above example demonstrates or define terms in context. Here is an example where the term "Chickens" is defined in context:

> Seller shall sell to Buyer 500 eviscerated frozen young chickens suitable for broiling and frying (the "**Chickens**").

It is common for a contract to define some terms in context and some terms in a definition section.

When defining a term, the convention is to capitalize the term and put it in quotes. Many drafters also bold or underline the term where it is defined to aid the reader in locating the definition. To signify that you are using a previously defined term in the contract, you simply capitalize the word (you do not put it in quotes, bold it, or underline it).

Don't get carried away with using defined terms. If a concept only appears once in a contract, there is no need to create a defined term for it. Further, it is unnecessary to define a term that has a well settled meaning (assuming you're using the term in its normal sense). For example, defining "Month" as "each of the twelve named periods into

which a year is divided" is overkill.   Just go
with the undefined term "month."

V.   THE CONTRACT DRAFTING
PROCESS

To give you a sense for how contracts are
drafted in practice, this part provides a description of a typical contract drafting process. For more routine commercial transactions, the process often starts with a call or
email from a client along the lines of: "We've
worked out a deal with TCB to supply us
with widgets. Draw up the contract, but
don't spend a lot of time on it." The client
will then presumably give you a rundown of
the basic terms of the deal. At this stage, you
want to get enough information so that you
can prepare a first draft of the contract. The
things you will need to know include amount
and specification of goods to be provided,
price to be paid, transport and delivery details, timing and form of payment, and duration of the deal.

If the client does not provide sufficient detail, you need to ask for it. You should also
ask him or her to forward you any documents relating to the transaction such as a
proposal letter or TCB marketing materials.
These documents may give you a better
sense for what exactly TCB is promising and
alert you to aspects of the deal not mentioned by the client that should be reflected
in the contract. Additionally, you should ask

the client how much he or she is thinking for legal fees on the project and how quickly the contract needs to be finalized (including when they would like to get the first draft from you). This allows you to meet or exceed client expectations on cost and timing or explain upfront why those expectations are not reasonable.

Once you have sufficient information to begin drafting, the next step is to locate a form or sample contract (often called a precedent) to use as the starting point for your contract. Rarely, if ever, do lawyers draft contracts from scratch. Instead, they revise and tailor contracts from other deals. Ideally, you will have drafted or reviewed a widget contract before that you can use as your precedent. If not, you can ask other attorneys in your firm if they have a sample. If you come up empty, you could check contract form books (available at most law libraries), search contract form databases on Westlaw or Lexis, or do a Google search. The worst case is that you start with a supply contract for some other type of goods, i.e., something other than widgets, and convert it to a widget supply contract. This may involve pulling widget specific language and provisions you located in a forms book or a Westlaw/Lexis/Google search. Do not, however, assume that any of the forms or samples you find are well drafted or complete. Once you gain expertise in drafting contracts, you may be surprised by how many poorly drafted contracts are in circulation, including those found in form books and databases. In other words, do not blindly adhere to a precedent or pull language from a form book. To improve your contract's clarity and precision, always scrutinize the language and redraft it as necessary.

You should try to use a precedent drafted by the attorney for the party that is on the same side of the transaction as your client (in our example, that would be the attorney for the party buying the widgets). This is because on a number of issues, the contracting parties will be diametrically opposed.

For example, a supplier of goods will want to provide minimal express representations and warranties with respect to the goods, disclaim implied warranties, cap damages for breach, and limit remedies. Conversely, a buyer will want broad representations and warranties and no warranty disclaimers, cap on damages, or limitations on remedies. Thus, if you represent the seller, it is best to start with a seller-drafted precedent because it will presumably include warranty disclaimers, damages cap, etc. Also, it may include seller favorable provisions that you otherwise would not have thought of including in the contract.

You prepare the first draft by revising and tailoring the precedent to reflect your specific deal. You then have your draft reviewed by a supervising attorney (if applicable) and incorporate his or her changes. Next, you send your draft to your client for their review and incorporate any comments they may have. Once your client has signed-off, you send the draft to the other side's attorney.

The other side will get back to you with some comments, and you discuss with your client (and perhaps your supervising attorney) how to respond. You then revise your draft to reflect the comments from the other side you have accepted and send the revised draft to the opposing attorney. The standard practice is to send a marked-to-show changes version (also called a red-line or blackline) and a clean version (you can create a marked-to-show changes version by using the "compare" feature of MS word).

Negotiations will ensue between you and the opposing attorney to resolve the comments you rejected. Presumably at some point all comments will be resolved, and you will prepare a final version of the contract for the parties to sign.

VI.   REVIEWING A CONTRACT

Oftentimes, you will not be the one drafting a contract but instead will be asked to review one drafted by the other side's attorney. This part provides some thoughts on reviewing a contract.

The reviewing process starts very similarly to the drafting process with an email or call from the client along the lines of the following: "We've worked out a deal to supply EFG with widgets. Their counsel is drawing up the contract, and she will be forwarding it to you shortly for review. We're anxious to get this finalized, so please turn it around quickly." The client will then presumably give you a rundown of the business terms of the deal. You need the same type of information you would need if you were drafting the contract so that you know what is supposed to be in the contract when reviewing it. Thus, if the client does not tell you the price to be paid, transport and delivery details, etc., you should ask. Do not assume that the client will review the draft and flag erroneous business terms. For a variety of reasons, clients often do not carefully read draft contracts (if at all), so it is your responsibility to make sure all business terms are correct. You should also ask for the name and contact information of the drafting attorney so that you can touch base with him or her ("Hi, this is _____. I represent TCB on the EFG widget deal. I look forward to working with you. . . . "), especially given your client is "anxious to get this finalized." Further, as you would do when drafting, you should ask the client to forward you any documents relating to the transaction (e.g., proposal letters, marketing materials) as these will give you a better understanding of the deal and presumably will be in the hands of opposing counsel.

While waiting for the first draft to hit your inbox, you should secure one or more sample contracts of similar deals, preferably early drafts prepared by seller's counsel since you represent the seller in this deal, and read through them. Doing so will give you a sense for standard provisions for these types of deals. More importantly, reading through samples will help you spot seller favorable provisions that the drafter of the contract you'll be reviewing has left out. This gets back to the point I made earlier that parties are often diametrically opposed on various issues. For example, EFG's attorney is unlikely to include in the draft a disclaimer of the implied warranty of merchantability because it is to her client's advantage for it not to be disclaimed. You may have forgotten about UCC § 2–314,[6] but your memory will be jogged when reading a sample contract that includes a warranty disclaimer, and you will then know to ask that one be added to the EFG contract if it is not in the initial draft.

---

[6] UCC § 2–314 provides, in relevant part: "Unless excluded or modified (Section 2–316), a warranty that the goods shall be merchantable is implied in a contract for their sale if the seller is a merchant with respect to goods of that kind."

There is no standard way to review a draft. Most people develop their own styles. Below I describe my style which may or may not work for you, but at least it will give you a sense for the review process.

1. Give the draft a quick read upon receipt to get a sense for how well it is drafted and how it is organized. My main objective here is to assess how much time I'll need to work through it.

2. Scrutinize the draft line by line noting drafting errors, ambiguities, inconsistencies, typos, etc. I do this by printing out the draft and handwriting changes on it much as a proofreader does (attorneys call this "marking up" a draft). In fact, some attorneys use the standard proofreader's marks for this step (google "proofreader marks" to find a listing).

3. Give the draft another close read, but this time focus on what is missing. Draft language for provisions you want added. Some attorneys will simply write "add implied warranty disclaimer" on a draft. The problem with this approach is that it might not be clear to the draftsperson what exactly you want, or he or she may use language that doesn't go as far as you want. I normally type up language I want added in a separate word document as opposed to handwriting it on the draft. I then label each provision sequentially

as "Rider 1," "Rider 2," etc. and indicate on the draft where I want each rider inserted.

4. If the draft contains complicated specialized provisions (for example, those addressing intellectual property, tax, or employee benefits), consider having someone with expertise in the relevant area review them.

5. Set the draft aside for a day and then give it another close read to make sure you caught everything.

The next step is to share your mark-up with the client and your supervising attorney (if applicable) to see if they have any questions or thoughts regarding your comments or comments of their own to add. You may want to do a cover memo for the client to draw attention to particular sections you want him or her to focus on or that asks specific questions.

Once the client and supervising attorney sign off, you then transmit your comments to the other side. My preference is to email a scan of my mark-up along with a word file of my riders with the hope that the drafter will just copy and paste the riders into the contract. Depending on the extent and complexity of my comments, I may then do a conference call with the drafter to walk him or her through them. Some reviewing attorneys do formal comment memos specifying and explaining each comment, but I find this method inefficient because the memo takes a long

time to draft and usually comments on the
mark-up are self explanatory, especially to
an experienced drafter. Thus, I only do one if
that is what the client (or supervising attorney) expect. Occasionally, I'll include an ex-
planation of a comment I think may be con-
troversial or not well received in the body of
the email transmitting the mark-up.

As mentioned above, the draftsperson will
make changes to the contract in response to
your comments but undoubtedly will reject
some of them. You then need to get feedback
from your client as to whether to push for
one or more of the rejected changes and pro-
ceed accordingly. A client will normally ask
what you think on pushing for a particular
comment, so you should think through your
answer and reasoning in advance.

VII.   CONCLUSION

This Introduction is designed to teach you
some basic principles of contract drafting
and is by no means comprehensive. Regardless, you do not learn to draft contracts by
reading articles or books about contract
drafting. You learn by drafting, reviewing,
and revising contracts. Because you do not
do much of that in law school, no one expects
you to be great at drafting right out of
school. Hopefully, you can take what you
have learned here to draft respectable contracts from day one and accelerate your

learning curve towards becoming a contract
drafting expert.

Exercise 1.

A.   Read the following contract and label the various components, e.g., preamble, recitals, representations and warranties, etc. (see section II. above).

B.   What changes to the contract would you request if you represented Barbosa?

C.   Yacht World has agreed to include a used 2008 Avon dinghy (a dinghy is a small boat carried on a large boat used to ferry people to and from where the large boat is anchored and the shore) in the deal for an extra $500. Mark-up the contract accordingly. "Mark-up" means cross out/handwrite changes on the contract. Assume you represent Yacht World.

WKS Draft 8/12/12

YACHT SALE AGREEMENT

Yacht Sale Agreement, dated _____, 2013, between Yacht World Co., a Delaware corporation ("**Seller**"), and Mia K. Barbosa, an individual residing at _____ ("**Buyer**").

Background

This Agreement provides for the sale of a yacht by Seller to Buyer.

Accordingly, the parties agree as follows:

1. **Definitions**. Terms defined in the preamble have their assigned meanings, and the following terms have the meanings assigned to them.

(a) "**Agreement**" means this Yacht Sale Agreement, as amended from time to time.

(b) "**Closing**" means the consummation of the transactions that this Agreement contemplates.

(c) "**Closing Date**" has the meaning assigned to it in Section 4.

(d) "**Purchase Price**" has the meaning assigned to it in Section 3.

(e) "**Yacht**" means the 2004 Hatteras model _____, name _____, hull # _____.

2. **Purchase and Sale**. At the Closing, Seller shall sell the Yacht to Buyer, and Buyer shall purchase it from Seller.

3. **Purchase Price**. At the Closing, Buyer shall pay Seller $5,600,000 (the "**Purchase Price**") by certified check.

4. **Time and Place of the Closing**. The Closing shall take place on _____, 2013, or such other date as to which the parties agree (the "**Closing Date**") at Seller's offices at 2:00 p.m. local time.

5. **Seller's Closing Deliveries**.

(a) **Documents**. At the Closing, Seller shall execute and deliver to Buyer a bill of sale for the Yacht. On the reasonable request of Buyer, either at or after the Closing, Seller shall execute and deliver to Buyer any other instrument necessary to vest Buyer with good title in the Yacht.

(b) **Yacht, Keys, and Manuals**. At the Closing, Seller shall deliver the Yacht, its keys, and owner's manuals to Buyer.

6. **Seller's Representations and Warranties**. Seller represents and warrants to Buyer as follows:

(a) **Ownership**. Seller owns the Yacht, and the Yacht is not subject to any liens, claims, or encumbrances.

(b) **Maintenance**. Seller has maintained the Yacht in accordance with the Yacht's owner's manual, and the Yacht is in good operating condition, normal wear and tear excepted.

(c) **DISCLAIMER OF WARRANTIES**. EXCEPT AS EXPRESSLY PROVIDED IN THIS SECTION 6., SELLER MAKES NO REPRESENTATION OR WARRANTY, EXPRESS OR IMPLIED, WITH RESPECT TO THE YACHT, INCLUDING, BUT NOT LIMITED TO, IMPLIED CONDITIONS OF FITNESS FOR A PARTICULAR PURPOSE, MERCHANTABILITY, WARRANTIES ARISING FROM COURSE

OF DEALING OR USAGE OF TRADE OR
ANY OTHER MATTER. NO AGENT,
EMPLOYEE OR REPRESENTATIVE OF
SELLER HAS ANY AUTHORITY TO
BIND SELLER TO ANY AFFIRMATION,
REPRESENTATION OR WARRANTY
EXCEPT AS STATED IN THIS AGREE-
MENT.

7. **Buyer's Representations and Warranties**. Buyer represents and warrants to
Seller as follows:

(a) **Financial Information**. The financial information of Buyer furnished to
Seller is accurate and complete and fairly
presents the financial position of Buyer as
of the date of such information.

(b) **Funding**. Buyer has sufficient funds
to pay the Purchase Price to Seller at Closing.

8. **Seller's Covenants**. Seller covenants
as follows from the date of this Agreement to
the Closing:

(a) **Use of the Yacht**. The Yacht shall
not be run for more than ___ hours.

(b) **Maintenance**. Seller shall maintain
the Yacht until the Closing in accordance
with the Yacht's owner's manual, and in
good operating condition, normal wear and
tear excepted.

9. **Conditions to Buyer's Obligations**. Buyer's obligation to close the transaction contemplated by this Agreement is subject to the satisfaction of the following conditions:

(a) **Representations and Warranties**. Seller's representations and warranties must be true on the Closing Date.

(b) **Covenants**. Seller must have performed all of the covenants to be performed by it on or before the Closing Date.

10. **Condition to Seller's Obligations**. Seller's obligation to close the transaction contemplated by this Agreement is subject to the satisfaction of the condition that Buyer's representation and warranties must be true on the Closing Date.

11. **Miscellaneous**.

(a) **Entire Agreement**. This Agreement is the final, complete, and exclusive statement of the parties' agreement on the matters contained in this Agreement and supersedes all prior communications, understandings and agreements between the parties related thereto.

(b) **Modification and Waiver**. No purported amendment, modification or waiver of any provision of this Agreement shall be binding unless set forth in a writing signed by both parties (in the case of amendments and modifications) or by the party to be charged (in the case of waivers). Any waiver shall be limited to the circumstance or event specifically referenced in the written waiver document and shall not be deemed a waiver of any other term of this Agreement or of the same circumstance or event upon any recurrence thereof.

(c) **Governing Law**. This Agreement shall be governed by and construed in accordance with the laws of the State of Washington without regard to the rules of conflict of laws of such state or any other jurisdiction.

(d) **Confidentiality**. Buyer agrees to keep the terms of this Agreement confidential.

To evidence the parties' agreement to this Agreement's provisions, they have executed and delivered this Agreement on the date set forth in the preamble.

YACHT WORLD CO.

By:_____

Its:_____

_____

Mia K. Barbosa

Exercise 2.

Fabco Inc., one of your clients, is a manufacturer of large industrial machinery. You
have received the following voicemail from
Bravo, Fabco's VP of operations:

"We've worked out a deal with Express
Transport to haul and deliver our products. I
need you to draft the contract. Give me a call
to discuss."

Prepare a list of questions for you to reference during your call with Bravo regarding
the contract.

Exercise 3.

Mark-up the following contract to correct errors and improve clarity and precision. Also, identify provisions or concepts that are likely missing from the contract.

CONSULTING AGREEMENT

This Agreement is entered into to be effective as of the ___ day of _____, 2013, by and between Edgester Co., a corporation incorporated under the laws of the state of Nevada, 7511 76th Street, Las Vegas, Nevada, 89117 (hereinafter, the Consultee or Edgester) and Nancy Smith, 15 Pilot Drive, Phoenix, Arizona, 85003 ("Consultant" or Smith).

WITNESSETH:

WHEREAS, the Consultant desires to provide to Consultee the services specified on Appendix A hereto (the "**Services**") and shall do so in a professional manner;

WHEREAS, Consultee desires to retain Consultant to provide such services as an independent contractor;

WHEREAS, the Consultee and the Consultant mutually desire to enter into this written Agreement which sets out the terms under which Consultant will perform such services.

AGREEMENT:

In consideration of the mutual covenants set forth herein and other good and valuable consideration, the receipt and sufficiency of which is hereby acknowledged, the parties agree as follows:

1. <u>Duties and Responsibilities</u>. Consultant agrees to use her best efforts in performing the Services.

2. <u>Compensation</u>. As compensation in full for the services rendered by Consultant hereunder, Consultant shall be paid $50 per Hour (the "Compensation"). "Hour" shall mean a period of time equal to a twenty-fourth part of a day and night and divided into 60 minutes.

3. <u>Title and Ownership</u>. Consultant acknowledges that her contribution to up-date, revise and create the Materials is specifically for the use by the Company, that such Materials shall be deemed to be "work made for hire" for purposes of the provisions of U.S. Copyright Act of 1976, 17 U.S.C. Section 1 <u>et</u>. <u>Seq</u>. (1976), as amended and that the Materials shall be the exclusive property of the Company. If the Materials should, for whatever reason, be deemed not to be "work made for hire", Consultant hereby assigns to the Company all of his right, title and interest in and to the Materials, including, without limitation, all copyright interest in the Materials. Consultant agrees to execute all

documents as may be reasonably requested by the Company to document the Company's ownership of the Materials.

4. In performing services for the Academy, Consultant may be exposed to and work with the Academy's confidential information including but not limited to student records, test results, and health information. Consultant acknowledges that he will keep any such information in strict confidence and shall not, directly or indirectly, reproduce, publish, disclose, use, reveal, show, or otherwise communicate or disclose to any person or entity any such confidential information.

5. <u>Independent Contractor</u>. Consultant is and shall remain an independent contractor and is not and shall not be deemed to be an employee of the Company. Accordingly, Consultant shall have no authority or right under any circumstance whatsoever to incur any indebtedness in the name of the Company or otherwise bind or purport to bind the Company in any manner whatsoever. Consultant shall be solely responsible for compliance with all applicable laws with respect to worker's compensation, withholding taxes, unemployment compensation, social security payments and all other charges against compensation imposed by any governmental authority. Neither this Agreement nor the relationship between the par-

ties constitutes a franchise, partnership or joint venture.

7. General Provisions.

(1) This Agreement represents the entire contract between the parties concerning the providing of consultant services to the Company by Smith and supersedes all prior agreements, whether written or oral, relating thereto.

(2) No purported amendment, modification or waiver of any provision of this Agreement shall be binding upon the parties hereto unless set forth in a written documents signed by all parties (in the case of amendments or modifications) or by the party to be charged thereby (in the case of waivers). Any waiver shall be limited to the circumstance or event specifically referenced in the written waiver document and shall not be deemed a waiver of any other term of this Agreement or of the same circumstance or event upon any recurrence thereof.

IN WITNESS WHEREOF the parties hereto have hereunto set their hands and seals the day and year first above written.

EDGSTER COMPANY

_____

Verona C. Gordon,
President

_____

Nancy G. Smith

Exercise 4.

Below are excerpts from the first draft of an acquisition agreement pursuant to which Seller is selling its business to Buyer. The draft was prepared by Buyer's counsel. Items 1-7 appear in a section titled "Seller's Representations and Warranties." Item 8 is from a section titled "Seller's Covenants." You represent Seller. Mark up the provisions with any changes you would request.

1. Seller owns all of its assets, or, in the cases of leases, valid and subsisting leasehold interests in the assets leased thereby, in each case free and clear of all liens, claims, and encumbrances. Seller has not received any notice of default under any lease and there is no event that, with notice or lapse of time or both, would constitute a default under any such lease.

2. None of Seller's rights to its intellectual property is being infringed, misused, or misappropriated by others.

3. Neither Seller nor its business, operations, products, or properties, currently or formerly owned, operated, or leased have violated or violate or have been or are subject to any judicial or administrative investigations, proceedings or other actions alleging the violation of, any federal, state, local or

foreign environmental, superfund, conserva-
tion, health or safety statute, regulation, or-
dinance, common law, order or decree.

4. There are no strikes, work stoppages or
controversies pending or threatened, between Seller and any of its employees.

5. Seller has not failed to file any reports
or tax returns required by any law or regulation of any jurisdiction to be filed as of the
date hereof, and all such reports and returns
are true and correct.

6. There are no debts, liabilities, claims
against or financial obligations of Seller, or
reasonable legal basis therefore, whether
accrued, absolute, contingent or otherwise,
except to the extent reflected on the balance
sheet of Seller dated December 31, 2012.

7. Since December 31, 2012, there has not
been any adverse change in the general affairs, management, net worth or condition
(financial or otherwise) of Seller or its business or assets.

8. As promptly as possible, Seller shall
take all corporate and other action, make all
filings with courts or governmental authori-
ties, and obtain in writing all approvals and
consents required to be obtained by Seller in
order to effectuate the Merger and the
transactions contemplated hereby.

Exercise 5.

You have decided to buy a used Porsche Carrera GT sports car from your neighbor, Jessie Desai. Make a list of representations and warranties you would like included in the car purchase agreement.

Exercise 6.

Prepare a contract for your purchase of the Porsche from Exercise 5. Use the Yacht Sale Agreement from Exercise 1. as your precedent.

Exercise 7.

Trade your contract from Exercise 6. with one or your classmates. Review and mark-up your classmate's contract as if you represent Desai.

APPENDIX

Below is an actual employment agreement drafted by an experienced attorney followed by a marked-to-show-changes version of the same agreement that reflects many of the lessons from this book. A lot of the changes are self-explanatory, but for some changes I've included footnotes with explanatory comments.

Assume that an associate representing the Company did the original draft of the contract and that the markup reflects changes made by the associate's supervisor. In other words, the markup generally reflects changes favorable to the Company.

Note that neither version is intended to serve as a precedent for an employment agreement. They are included in this book as examples only.

EMPLOYMENT AGREEMENT

EFFECTIVE DATE: April 1, 2012

PARTIES:

Kanix Inc.
123 Mountain Road
Golden, CO 80403   (the "Company")

Priya Singh
456 Valley Street
Denver, CO 80209   ("Employee")

RECITALS:

A. The Company is engaged in the nanotechnology business.

B. The Company, through its research, development and expenditure of funds, has developed confidential information, including trade secrets.

C. Employee desires to be employed by the Company and the Company desires to employ Employee under the terms and conditions of this Agreement.

D. During her employment, Employee will have access to the Company's valuable confidential information, may contribute to such confidential information and acknowledges that the Company will suffer irreparable harm if Employee uses confidential information outside her employment or makes unauthorized disclosure of confidential information to any third party.

E. Employee further recognizes that execution of this Agreement is an express condition of employment with the Company.

AGREEMENTS:

In consideration of the mutual covenants contained herein, and other good and valuable consideration, the receipt and sufficiency of which is hereby acknowledged, the parties agree as follows:

1. Employment. Subject to all of the terms and conditions of this Agreement, Employee agrees to devote her full time and best efforts to serving as vice president of research and development for the Company at such times, places and in such a manner as the Company directs.

2. Compensation.

a. Salary. The Company shall pay Employee a base salary of two hundred fifty thousand dollars ($250,000.00) per year. Payments shall be made to the Employee by Company check in accordance with the Company's normal payroll procedures.

b. Bonus. The Employee shall be entitled to an annual cash bonus in an amount to be determined by the Company.

c. Business Expenses. The Company shall reimburse Employee for all reasonable out-of-pocket and substantiated business expenses incurred by Employee in performing his duties hereunder.

d. <u>Other Benefits</u>. The Company shall provide to Employee participation in any other employee benefits or programs now existing or hereafter established by the Company for its employees in general.

3. <u>Term</u>. The term of this Agreement shall commence on the Effective Date first stated above and continue for a period of two (2) years (the "Initial Term") and shall automatically renew for successive one (1) year periods thereafter, until terminated pursuant to any of the following provisions:

a. <u>Delivery of Notice</u>. Employee may terminate this Agreement, with or without cause, by delivery of thirty (30) days advance written notice to the Company.

b. <u>Death</u>. This Agreement shall automatically terminate upon the death of Employee.

c. <u>Disability</u>. The Company may terminate this Agreement by delivery of written notice to Employee upon the physical or mental disability of Employee to such an extent that he is unable to continue to perform his duties determined under Section 1 of this Agreement for a continuous period of ninety (90) days.

d. <u>Criminal Action</u>. The Company may terminate this Agreement by delivery of written notice to Employee in the event of Employee's conviction of or entry of a plea of guilty or <u>nolo contendere</u> to any felony or misdemeanor or the entry of any final civil judgment against him in connection with any allegation of fraud, misrepresentation, misappropriation of property, any other intentional tort or violation of any statute which relates to the affairs of the Company.

e. Injurious Act. The Company may terminate this Agreement by delivery of written notice to Employee if Employee commits any willful, intentional or grossly negligent act which has the effect of injuring the reputation of the Company or materially injuring the business or performance of the Company.

4. Confidential Information.

a. Obligations. During her employment with the Company and at all times after termination of Employee's employment with the Company for whatever reason, Employee agrees not to directly or indirectly disclose to others or use any proprietary or Confidential Information or trade secrets of the Company or any subsidiary, whether obtained as a result, directly or indirectly, of her employment with the Company or otherwise. Employee agrees to refrain from such acts and omissions which would reduce the value of the Confidential Information to the Company. For purposes of this Agreement, "Confidential Information" shall include but shall not be limited to names and other information concerning clients and referral sources, software, business plans, techniques, and strategies, technical information, contracts, compilations of information, business records of any kind, health assessment tools and reports of any kind, and any other information that the

Company or its affiliates considers to be confidential or a trade secret and which the Company or its affiliates reasonably believes provides an opportunity to obtain an advantage over competitors who do not know such confidential information or trade secrets.

b. <u>Upon Termination</u>. Employee shall, immediately upon the termination of Employee's employment with the Company for whatever reason, deliver to the Company all documents and other items, including copies thereof, whether on computer disc or otherwise. within Employee's possession or control, belonging to the Company or in any way related to the business of the Company or the services Employee performed for the Company, including but not limited to any documents or items containing any Confidential Information within Employee's possession or control and any other materials or documents relating to product designs, manufacturing methods, processes, techniques, tooling, research and marketing, sales techniques, marketing plans or proposals, financial and sales information, existing, inactive or potential customer lists and all other customer information.

5. <u>Inventions</u>.

a. <u>Assignment</u>. Employee agrees to communicate promptly and fully to the Company all inventions, discoveries, improvements or designs conceived or reduced to practice by Employee during the period of her employment with the Company (alone or jointly with others), and, except as provided in Section 5.c., Employee will and hereby does assign to the Company and/or its nominees all of her right, title and interest in such inventions, discoveries, improvements or designs and all of her right, title and interest in any patents, patent applications or copyrights based thereon without obligation on the part of the Company to pay any further compensation, royalty or payment to Employee.

b. <u>Assistance</u>. Employee further agrees to assist the Company and/or its nominee (without charge but at no expense to Employee) at any time and in every proper way to obtain and maintain for its and/or their own benefit, patents for all such inventions, discoveries and improvements and copyrights for all such designs.

c. <u>Exclusions</u>. This Agreement does not obligate Employee to assign to the Company any invention, discovery, improvement or design for which no equipment, supplies, facility or trade secret information of the Company was used and which was developed entirely on Employee's own time, and (i) which does not relate (A) directly to the business of the Company or (B) to the Company's actual or demonstrably anticipated research or development, or (ii) which does not result from any work performed by Employee for the Company.

d. <u>Records</u>. Employee shall keep complete, accurate and authentic accounts, notes, data and records of all inventions, discoveries, improvements or designs in the manner and form requested by the Company. Such accounts, notes, data and records shall be the property of the Company, and upon its request Employee shall promptly surrender the same to the Company.

e. <u>Continuing Obligation after Termination of Employment</u>. The obligations of this Section 5 shall continue beyond the termination of Employee's employment with respect to any invention, discovery, improvement or design conceived or made by Employee during the period of Employee's employment with the Company and shall be binding upon Employee's assigns, executors, administrators, and other legal representatives. In the event Employee is called upon to render assistance to the Company pursuant to Section 5.b. after termination of Employee's employment with the Company, the Company shall pay Employee reasonable compensation for the assistance rendered and shall call upon Employee for assistance at such reasonable times so as not to interfere with Employee's new employment or business. For purposes of this Agreement, any invention, discovery, improvement or design relating to the business of the Company upon which Employee files a patent, trademark of copyright application within one (1) year after termination of Employee's employment with the Company shall be presumed to have been made while Employee was employed by the Company, subject to proof to the contrary by good faith, written and duly corroborated records establishing that such invention, discovery, improvement or design was conceived and made by Employee following termination of employment and without violation of her continuing obligations under Section 4 hereof.

6. Restrictive Covenants.

a. Noncompetition. During Employee's employment with the Company and for a period of one (1) year immediately following termination of Employee's employment with the Company, for whatever reason, Employee agrees not to directly or indirectly plan, organize or engage in any business which to any extent competes with any product or service marketed or planned for marketing by the Company or conspire with others to do so, whether as an owner, principal, partner, five percent (5%) or more shareholder, director, officer, employee, lender, sponsor, proprietary, joint venturer, agent, trustee, advisor or consultant.

b. Solicitation of Company Employees. During Employee's employment with the Company, and for a period of one (1) year immediately following the termination of Employee's employment with the Company, for whatever reason, Employee agrees not to solicit any Company employees, either directly or indirectly, to leave the employment of the Company.

c. Solicitation of Company Customers. For a period of one (1) year after termination of Employee's employment with the Company, Employee agrees not to attempt to divert or interfere with the development of any Company business by soliciting, contacting, or communicating with any person, firm, or organization to whom the Company sold or solicited the sale of the Company's services or products during the year preceding termination of Employee's employment with the Company for the purpose of providing a competing product.

7.   Effect of Termination of Employment - Compensation.   All compensation or other benefits to which the Employee is entitled hereunder shall cease upon the effective date of termination of her employment.   The Company shall be obligated to pay any unpaid wages for services performed and any unused and accrued vacation time as of the effective date of termination.   Employee shall have the right to purchase extended coverage under any of the Company's then-existing insurance plans, including, health, life and disability, to the extent allowable under such insurance policies.

8. General Provisions.

a. Remedy Upon Violation. Employee agrees that the Company shall be entitled, in addition to any other remedy it may have at law or in equity, to an injunction with the posting of the minimum allowable bond, enjoining or restraining Employee from any violation or violations of this Agreement, and Employee hereby consents to the issuance of such injunction. If any of the rights or restrictions contained in this Agreement shall be deemed to be unenforceable by reason of the extent, duration or geographic scope, or other provision hereof, then the parties hereto agree that the court shall reduce such extent, duration, geographic scope or other provision hereof and enforce the provisions in reduced form for all purposes in the manner contemplated hereby.

b. Obligations Which Survive Termination. The obligations of Employee in Sections 4, 5 and 6 hereof shall survive the execution and termination of this Agreement.

c. Assignment. The obligations contained in this agreement are personal as to Employee and Employee may not assign any of her rights hereunder; provided, however, that this Agreement shall be binding on Employee's heirs and legal representatives. The Company shall have the right to transfer its rights hereunder to its successors and assigns.

d. Notices. All notices permitted or required hereunder shall be in writing and shall be deemed to have been duly given (i) when received if delivered by hand, by telegram, or by teletype, (ii) one (1) business day after delivery by facsimile, (iii) two (2) business days after delivery by reputable overnight carrier, or (iv) three (3) business days after placement in the U.S. mails for delivery by registered or certified mail, return receipt requested, postage prepaid and addressed to the appropriate party at the address set forth on the first page hereof. Addresses may be changed by written notice given pursuant to this section but any such notice shall be effective only with actually received by the addressee.

e. <u>Modification and Waiver</u>. No purported amendment, modification or waiver of any provision of this Agreement shall be binding unless set forth in a written document signed by all parties (in the case of amendments or modifications) or by the party to be charged thereby (in the case of waivers). Any waiver shall be limited to the circumstance or event specifically referenced in the written waiver document and shall not be deemed a waiver of any other term of this Agreement or of the same circumstance or event upon any recurrence thereof.

f. <u>Governing Law</u>. This Agreement shall be governed by and construed in accordance with the laws of the State of Minnesota, without application of its conflict of laws principles.

g. <u>Entire Agreement</u>. This Agreement constitutes the entire agreement between the parties and supersedes any and all prior oral or written understandings between the parties relating to the subject matter hereof.

The parties hereto have executed this Agreement to be effective the day and year first above written.

_____

("Employee")

(the "Company")

By_____

Its_____

EMPLOYMENT AGREEMENT

~~EFFECTIVE DATE: April 1, 2012~~

~~PARTIES:~~

> ~~Kanix Inc.~~
> ~~123 Mountain Road~~
> ~~Golden, CO 80403~~   ~~(the "Company")~~

> ~~Priya Singh~~
> ~~456 Valley Street~~
> ~~Denver, CO 80209~~   ~~("Employee")~~

This Employment Agreement is dated April 1, 2012, and is between Kanix Inc., a Colorado corporation (the **"Company"**), and Priya K. Singh, an individual residing at 456 Valley Street, Denver, Colorado 80209 (**"Employee"**).[1]

~~RECITALS:~~**Background**[2]

~~A. The Company is engaged in the nanotechnology business.~~

~~B. The Company, through its research, development and expenditure of funds, has developed confidential information, including trade secrets.~~

---

[1] The original preamble was fine, but I prefer my version because it takes up less space, and there is no need to have Kanix's address in the preamble.

[2] The original recitals went well beyond providing context to the reader.

C. Employee desires to be employed by the
Company, and the Company desires to employ
Employee, under the terms and conditions of this
Agreement.

D. During her employment, Employee will
have access to the Company's valuable confidential information, may contribute to such confidential information and acknowledges that the Company will suffer irreparable harm if Employee
uses confidential information outside her employment or makes unauthorized disclosure of
confidential information to any third party.

E. Employee further recognizes that execution
of this Agreement is an express condition of employment with the Company.

AGREEMENTS:

In consideration of the mutual covenants contained herein, and other good and valuable consideration, the receipt and sufficiency of which is
hereby acknowledged Accordingly, the parties
agree as follows:

1. Employment. Subject to all of the terms and
conditions of this Agreement,Employee shall
serve as vice president of research and development for the Company at such times, places and
in such a manner as the Company directs and
shall perform all duties incident to such position
as well as any other duties as may from time to
time be assigned to her by the Company.[3]

---

[3] This language provides the Company with flexibility to use
Employee in a different role without arguably being in breach of

Empoyee shall devote her ~~full time and~~ best efforts, <u>energies, and skill in performing such duties, and to that end, shall devote her full time and attention exclusively to the business and affairs of the Company. Employee shall abide by all policies and rules of the Company.</u>

   2. <u>Compensation</u>.

      a.   <u>Base Salary</u>.   <u>During the term of this Agreement,</u> ~~T~~the Company shall pay Employee <u>at the rate of</u> ~~a base salary of two hundred fifty thousand dollars~~ ($250,000.00)[4] per ~~year~~ <u>annum</u>.[5] <u>The Company shall pay</u> ~~Payments shall be made to the~~ Employee ~~by Company check~~ in accordance with the Company's normal payroll procedures.[6]

      b.   <u>Bonus</u>.   ~~The~~[7]Employee shall be entitled to an annual cash bonus in an amount to be determined by the Company<u>, in its sole discretion.</u>

---

the Agreement. It also helps in defending against a constructive discharge claim following a change to Employee's duties.

   [4] Lawyers commonly spell out numbers and then follow them with Arabic numerals. This is unnecessary and therefore should be avoided. You should spell out numbers one through ten and use Arabic numerals for numbers over ten.

   [5] Employees have on occasion argued that the original language created a guarantee of employment for a year or guarantee of full pay for a year. Going with "at the rate of" eliminates these arguments.

   [6] I deleted the reference to "check" in case the Company wants to pay Employee by some other means, i.e., electronic funds transfer.

   [7] The defined term "Employee" is not preceded by "the" in the definition parenthetical so it should not be so preceded anywhere in the Agreement.

c. Business Expenses. The Company shall reimburse Employee for all reasonable out-of-pocket ~~and substantiated~~ business expenses incurred by Employee in performing ~~his~~ her duties ~~hereunder~~under this Agreement and submitted by Employee in accordance with the Company's reimbursement policy then in effect.

d. Vacation. Employee shall be entitled to 20 days of paid vacation during each year of her employment under this Agreement. Unused vacation shall not carry over to the next year.

~~d~~ e. Other Benefits. ~~The Company shall provide to~~ Employee shall be entitled to participat~~ion~~e in any ~~other~~ employee welfare and health benefit plans ~~or programs~~ now existing or hereafter established by the Company for its employees in general.

f. Withholdings. The Company may withhold from any salary or benefits payable to Employee all federal, state, local and other taxes and other amounts as permitted or required pursuant to law, rule or regulation.

3. Term. The term of this Agreement shall commence on the April 1, 2012 ~~Effective Date first stated above~~ and ~~continue for a period of two (2) years (the "Initial Term") and shall automatically renew for successive one (1) year periods thereafter~~ terminate on March 31, 2014, unless extended in writing by both the Company and

Employee ~~until~~ or earlier terminated pursuant to any of the following provisions:[8]

a. <u>Delivery of Notice</u>. Employee may terminate this Agreement, with or without cause, by delivery of ~~thirty~~(30) days advance written notice to the Company.

b. <u>Death</u>. This Agreement shall automatically terminate upon the death of Employee.

c. <u>Disability</u>. The Company may terminate this Agreement by delivery of written notice to Employee ~~upon~~ <u>following</u> the physical or mental disability of Employee to such an extent that<u>, in the Company's judgment,</u> she ~~is~~ <u>has been</u> unable to ~~continue to~~ perform ~~his~~ <u>her</u> duties ~~determined~~ under ~~Section 1 of~~ this Agreement for ~~a continuous period of ninety~~ (90) <u>consecutive</u> days.

d. <u>~~Criminal Action~~For Cause</u>. <u>The Company may terminate this Agreement at any time for Cause. For purposes of this Agreement, "**Cause**" includes, without limitation, (1) failure or neglect by Employee to perform the duties of the Employee's position; (2) failure of Employee to obey orders given by the Company or supervisors; (3) misconduct in connection with the performance of any of Employee's duties, including, without limitation, misappropriation of funds or property of the Company,</u>

---

[8] I generally try to avoid having contracts automatically renew because it can be a trap for the unwary. Additionally, in the employment context there is case law creating a presumption of renewal that can be overcome by the "unless extended in writing" language I added.

securing or attempting to secure personally any profit in connection with any transaction entered into on behalf of the Company, misrepresentation to the Company, or any violation of law or regulations on Company premises or to which the Company is subject; (4) commission by Employee of an act involving moral turpitude, dishonesty, theft or unethical business conduct, or conduct which impairs or injures the reputation of, or harms, the Company; (5) disloyalty by Employee, including, without limitation, aiding a competitor; (6) failure by Employee to work exclusively for the Company; and (7) any breach of this Agreement by Employee.[9] ~~The Company may terminate this Agreement by delivery of written notice to Employee in the event of Employee's conviction of or entry of a plea of guilty or nolo contendere to any felony or misdemeanor or the entry of any final civil judgment against him in connection with any allegation of fraud, misrepresentation, misappropriation of property, any other intentional tort or violation of any statute which relates to the affairs of the Company.~~

~~e. Injurious Act. The Company may terminate this Agreement by delivery of written notice to Employee if Employee commits any willful, intentional or grossly negligent act which has the effect of injuring the reputation of the~~

---

[9] It is important from the employer's perspective that an employment agreement for a term include a fairly broad termination provisions.   Thus, I expanded the list of circumstances under which the Company can terminate the Agreement.   I deleted subsection e. because it is subsumed by the new language of subsection d.

~~Company or materially injuring the business or performance of the Company.~~

4. Confidential Information.

a. Obligations. During her employment with the Company and at all times after termination of Employee's employment with the Company ~~for whatever reason~~, Employee agrees not to directly or indirectly disclose to others or use any proprietary or Confidential Information or trade secrets of the Company or any ~~subsidary~~ Company affiliate, whether obtained as a result, directly or indirectly, of her employment with the Company or otherwise. Employee agrees to refrain from such acts and omissions which would reduce the value of the Confidential Information to the Company. For purposes of this Agreement, "**Confidential Information**" ~~shall~~ includes, but ~~shall~~ is not ~~be~~ limited to, names and other information concerning clients and referral sources, software, business plans, research, techniques, and strategies, technical information, contracts, compilations of information, business records ~~of any kind, health assessment tools and reports of any kind~~, and any other information that the Company or its affiliates considers to be confidential or a trade secret and which the Company or its affiliates reasonably believes provides an opportunity to obtain an advantage over competitors who do not know such confidential information or trade secrets.

b. Upon Termination. Employee shall, immediately upon the termination of ~~Employee's~~

~~employment with the Company for whatever reason~~ this Agreement, deliver to the Company all documents and other items, including copies thereof, whether on computer disc or otherwise, within Employee's possession or control, belonging to the Company or in any way related to the business of the Company or the services Employee performed for the Company, including but not limited to any documents or items containing any Confidential Information within Employee's possession or control and any other materials or documents relating to product designs, manufacturing methods, processes, techniques, tooling, research and marketing, sales techniques, marketing plans or proposals, financial and sales information, existing, inactive or potential customer lists and all other customer information.

5. <u>Inventions</u>.

a. <u>Assignment</u>. Employee agrees to communicate promptly and fully to the Company all inventions, discoveries, improvements or designs conceived or reduced to practice by Employee during the period of her employment with the Company (alone or jointly with others), and, except as provided in Section 5.c., Employee will and hereby does assign to the Company and/or its nominees all of her right, title and interest in such inventions, discoveries, improvements or designs and all of her right, title and interest in any patents, patent applications or copyrights based thereon without obligation on the part of the Company to pay any further compensation, royalty or payment to Employee.

b. <u>Assistance</u>. Employee further agrees to assist the Company and/or its nominee (without charge but at no expense to Employee) at any time and in every proper way to obtain and maintain for its and/or their own benefit, patents for all such inventions, discoveries and improvements and copyrights for all such designs.

c. <u>Exclusions</u>. This Agreement does not obligate Employee to assign to the Company any invention, discovery, improvement or design for which no equipment, supplies, facility or trade secret information of the Company was used and which was developed entirely on Employee's own time, and (1~~i~~) which does not relate (A) directly to the business of the Company or (B) to the Company's actual or demonstrably anticipated research or development, or (2~~ii~~)[10] which does not result from any work performed by Employee for the Company.

d. <u>Records</u>. Employee shall keep complete, accurate and authentic accounts, notes, data and records of all inventions, discoveries, improvements or designs in the manner and form requested by the Company. Such accounts, notes, data and records shall be the property of the Company, and upon its request Employee shall promptly surrender the same to the Company.

---

[10] I changed these romanettes to numerals to match the numbering format I used earlier in § 3.d.

e. <u>Continuing Obligation after Termination ~~of Employment~~</u>. The obligations of this Section 5 shall continue beyond the termination of ~~Employee's employment~~ <u>this Agreement</u> with respect to any invention, discovery, improvement or design conceived or made by Employee during the period of Employee's employment with the Company and shall be binding upon Employee's assigns, executors, administrators, and other legal representatives. In the event Employee is called upon to render assistance to the Company pursuant to Section 5.b. after termination of Employee's employment with the Company, the Company shall pay Employee reasonable compensation for the assistance rendered and shall call upon Employee for assistance at such reasonable times so as not to interfere with Employee's new employment or business. For purposes of this Agreement, any invention, discovery, improvement or design relating to the business of the Company upon which Employee files a patent, trademark of copyright application within one ~~(1)~~ year after termination of ~~Employee's employment with the Company~~ <u>this Agreement</u> shall be presumed to have been made while Employee was employed by the Company, subject to proof to the contrary by good faith, written and duly corroborated records establishing that such invention, discovery, improvement or design was conceived and made by Employee following termination of employment and without violation of her continuing obligations under Section 4 hereof.

6. <u>Restrictive Covenants</u>.

a. <u>Noncompetition</u>. During ~~Employee's employment with the Company and~~ <u>the term of this Agreement and</u> for <u>the one-year</u> ~~a~~ period ~~of one (1) year~~ immediately following termination of ~~Employee's employment with the Company, for whatever reason~~ <u>this Agreement</u>, Employee ~~agrees~~ <u>shall</u> not ~~to~~ directly or indirectly plan, organize or engage in any business which to any extent competes with ~~any product or service marketed or planned for marketing by~~ the Company or conspire with others to do so, whether as an owner, principal, partner, ~~five percent (5%) or more~~ shareholder, director, officer, <u>member</u>, employee, lender, sponsor, ~~proprietary,~~ joint venturer, agent, trustee, advisor<u>,</u> ~~or~~ consultant <u>or otherwise</u>.

b. <u>Solicitation of Company Employees</u>. During ~~Employee's employment with the Company~~ <u>the term of this Agreement</u>, and for ~~a period of one (1)~~ <u>the one</u> year <u>period</u> immediately following the termination of ~~Employee's employment with the Company, for whatever reason~~ <u>this Agreement</u>, Employee ~~agrees~~ <u>shall</u> not ~~to~~ <u>employ or attempt to employ or assist anyone in employing any person who is an employee of the Company or was an employee of the Company during the previous one year period</u> ~~solicit any Company employees, either directly or indirectly, to leave the employment of the Company~~.

c. <u>Solicitation of Company Customers</u>. For <u>the one year period</u> ~~a period of one (1) year after~~ immediately <u>following</u> termination of ~~Employee's employment with the Company~~ <u>this</u>

Agreement, Employee ~~agrees~~ <u>shall</u> not ~~to~~ attempt to divert or interfere with the development of any Company business by soliciting, contacting, or communicating with any person, firm, or organization to whom the Company sold or solicited the sale of the Company's services or products during the ~~year preceding termination of Employee's employment with the Company~~ <u>previous one year period</u> for the purpose of providing a competing product <u>or</u> <u>service</u>.

7.   <u>Effect of Termination of Employment—</u> <u>Compensation</u>. All compensation or other benefits to which the Employee is entitled ~~hereunder~~ <u>to under this Agreement</u> shall cease upon ~~the effective date of termination of her employment~~ <u>termination of this Agreement</u>. The Company shall be obligated to pay any unpaid wages for services performed and any unused and accrued vacation time as of the effective date of <u>such</u> termination. Employee shall have the right to purchase extended coverage under any of the Company's then-existing insurance plans, including, health, life and disability, to the extent allowable under such insurance policies.

8.   <u>Representations and Warranties of Employ-</u> <u>ee. Employee represents and warrants to the</u> <u>Company as follows:</u>[11]

---

[11] The original had no representations and warranties, a glaring omission. Thus, I added this section. Note that per § 3.d.(7), the Company can terminate this Agreement if it turns out that one of these reps is false.

a. Legal Capacity. Employee has the legal capacity and unrestricted right to execute and deliver this Agreement and to perform all of her obligations under this Agreement.

b. No Conflicts. The execution and delivery of this Agreement by Employee and the performance of her obligations under this Agreement will not violate or be in conflict with any fiduciary or other duty, instrument, agreement, document, arrangement or other understanding to which Employee is a party or by which she is or may be bound or subject.

c. No Restrictions. Employee is not a party to any instrument, agreement, document, arrangement or other understanding with any person (other than the Company) requiring or restricting the use or disclosure of any confidential information or the provision of any employment, consulting or other services.

89. General Provisions.

a. Remedy Upon Violation. Employee ~~agrees~~ acknowledges that the Company shall be entitled, in addition to any other remedy it may have at law or in equity, to an injunction with the posting of the minimum allowable bond, enjoining or restraining Employee from any violation or violations of this Agreement, and Employee hereby consents to the issuance of such injunction. If any of the rights or restrictions contained in this Agreement ~~shall be~~ are deemed to be unenforceable by reason of the extent, duration or geographic scope, or other provision hereof, then the parties ~~hereto~~ to this

Agreement agree that the court shall reduce such extent, duration, geographic scope or other provision hereof and enforce the provisions in reduced form for all purposes in the manner contemplated hereby.

b.   Obligations Which Survive Termination. The obligations of Employee in Sections 4, 5 and 6 ~~hereof~~ of this Agreement shall survive ~~the~~ its execution and termination ~~of this Agreement~~.

c.   Assignment. ~~The obligations contained in this agreement are personal as to Employee and~~ Employee may not assign any of her rights or delegate any of her duties under this Agreement. Any attempted assignment or delegation by Employee shall be void.   Notwithstanding the foregoing, ~~hereunder; provided, however that~~ this Agreement shall be binding on Employee's heirs and legal representatives. ~~The Company shall have the right to transfer its rights hereunder to its successors and assigns.~~

d.   Notices.   All notices permitted or required ~~here~~under this Agreement shall be in writing and shall be deemed to have been duly given (1~~i~~) when received if delivered by hand~~, by telegram, or by teletype,~~ (2~~ii~~) one ~~(1)~~ business day after ~~delivery~~ being sent by facsimile or email to the applicable fax number or email address listed below, (3~~iii~~) two ~~(2)~~ business days after delivery by reputable overnight carrier, or (4~~iv~~) three ~~(3)~~ business days after placement in the U.S. mails for delivery by registered or certified mail, return receipt requested, postage prepaid and addressed ~~to the appropriate party at the address set forth on the first page hereof~~ as specified below. Addresses may be changed by written notice given pursuant to this section but any such notice shall be effective only with actually received by the addressee.[12]

Company contact information	Employee contact information
Kanix Inc.	Priya Singh
Attention: Human Resources	Address listed in the preamble
123 Mountain Road	Fax: 303-555-5555
Golden, CO 80403	
	Email:
	priya.singh@bmail.com
Fax: 720-555-5555	
Email: hr@kanix.com	

    e. <u>Modification and Waiver</u>. No purported amendment, modification or waiver of any provision of this Agreement shall be binding unless set forth in a written document signed by all parties (in the case of amendments or modifications) or by the party to be charged thereby (in the case of waivers). Any waiver shall be limited to the circumstance or event specifically referenced in the written waiver document and shall not be deemed a waiver of any other term

---

[12] It is fairly common to run across notice provisions that reference telegrams and teletype. Nobody provides notice by these means anymore so I deleted them. I also added a reference to notice by email.

of this Agreement or of the same circumstance or event upon any recurrence thereof.

f. <u>Governing Law</u>. This Agreement shall be governed by and construed in accordance with the laws of the State of ~~Minnesota~~ <u>Colorado</u>, without application of its conflict of laws principles.

g. <u>Entire Agreement</u>. This Agreement ~~constitutes~~ <u>is the final, complete, and exclusive statement of</u> ~~the entire agreement between~~ the parties' <u>agreement on the matters contained in this Agreement</u> and supersedes ~~any and~~ all prior ~~oral or written~~ <u>communications,</u> understandings <u>and agreements</u> between the parties relating to the subject matter ~~hereof~~ <u>of this Agreement.</u>

<u>To evidence the parties' agreement to this Agreement's provisions, they have executed and delivered this Agreement on the date set forth in the preamble.</u> ~~The parties hereto have executed this Agreement to be effective the day and year first above written.~~

_____

Priya K. Singh~~("Employee")~~

Kanix Inc.~~(the "Company")~~

By_____

Its_____